Interactive Mental Maths

working with the whole class **1**

Peter Patilla

For Year 1 (Level 2) / Primary 2 (Level A and above)

Heinemann Educational Publishers
Halley Court, Jordan Hill, Oxford, OX2 8EJ
a division of Reed Educational and Professional Publishing Ltd

Heinemann is a registered trademark of Reed Educational and Professional Publishing Ltd

OXFORD MELBOURNE AUCKLAND
JOHANNESBURG BLANTYRE GABORONE
IBADAN PORTSMOUTH (NH) CHICAGO

First published 1999

03 02 01 00 99
10 9 8 7 6 5 4 3 2

ISBN 0 435 02502 3

Designed, typeset and illustrated by AMR
Cover design by Tokay
Cover illustrations by Nick Sharratt
Printed and bound in Great Britain by George Over Limited, Rugby and London

Acknowledgements

I wish to thank all the pupils and their teachers who have contributed to the ideas in this book by
trialling and working on the activities over the past few years. They have helped develop many of my
original thoughts. My thanks also to teaching and publishing colleagues for their advice, ideas
and support.

Many of the activities have been influenced by authors who have written about maths education and
how children learn. I am grateful for their research in this area.

The 'Birthday Song' on page 40 was written by Hannah and Ann Broadbent. Thanks for allowing me
to use their song.

The flip-flop idea originated in *Number Work for Infants* by A. Thomas and M. Bannister published by
Blackwell in 1974.

Enthusiasm for clapping games was encouraged by Mary Baratta-Lorton in *Mathematics Their Way*,
published by Addison Wesley.

Much support was given by Sally Breedon of NES Arnold in producing and providing resources for
use in the development of some of the ideas used in this series of books.

Finally, thank you to Thomas and Joseph Shipman, young number enthusiasts, who provided the
motivation for collecting all these ideas together.

Peter Patilla

Contents

Introduction

The *Interactive Mental Maths* series is designed to support the implementation of the National Numeracy Strategy and Early Intervention Project. Each book contains activities suitable for regular 10 minute sessions with the whole class before the main teaching activity. The mental mathematics skills develop from book to book often using the same techniques to build up familiarity, comfort and the all-important practice. Timetable 'menus' are provided to assist planning.

Interactive Mental Maths 1 systematically develops three aspects of mental mathematics:

- **Quick recall of facts**   Pupils need to develop their maths knowledge in order to quickly recall facts. This includes number facts such as addition and subtraction bonds to 10. It also includes immediate recognition of small quantities. Quick recall can also include telling the time.

- **Mental calculations**   Pupils need efficient techniques to make mental calculations without resorting to formal taught algorithms. Examples include quick additions and subtractions of 1 and 10 as well as adding and subtracting small numbers to and from larger numbers.

- **Mental problem solving**   Pupils need to be able to solve word problems and more complex mental calculations where the operation required might not be immediately obvious. They should learn to solve non-routine problems and know the operations needed to answer them.

Interactive techniques

The suggestions included throughout the book focus upon interactive techniques suitable for direct teaching, usually to a whole class and occasionally to a large group. Lively and appropriate questions, explanations and illustrations are all used to make mathematics interactive, and ensure that all pupils have the opportunity to explain and illustrate their methods to you and to fellow pupils. Mathematics can also be made participatory by using techniques and strategies to ensure that all pupils take part in the activities to the best of their abilities.

The three teaching devices below will build pupils' confidence and encourage them to take part in whole-class activities.

- **Big Circle time**   Pupils sit in a large circle with you and have full eye contact with each other. This will help them to co-operate more and there will be fewer distractions. Your questioning will be more evenly spread.

- **Show me**   Pupils hold up number cards and other simple pieces of apparatus. The format of the activity ensures that everyone takes part. A glance round the responses is a quick and efficient way of assessment. This activity builds up pupils self-confidence and is an alternative to 'called out' answers. It also gives pupils time to think.

- **Number lines**   Active number lines such as human number lines, number washing lines and counting sticks ensure pupil interaction and develop a realization that numbers can be moved and rearranged.

Using the books

Interactive Mental Maths 1 is organized into two-page units, each with a main heading indicating the key skill(s) covered by the activities included. The purpose of the activities, and suggestions for development are shown at the top of the left-hand page.

The activities have been chosen for their high 'repeat value' with a particular year group – in other words, they lend themselves to being used on several occasions.

You may choose one or more activities from the same two-page unit for use on different days during a week. Alternatively, you may prefer to vary the activities presented to the children. In this instance, the timetable 'menus' on pages 7–9 can be used to assist with planning.

Skills development

By the end of the activities in this book, pupils should have acquired skills in the following areas.

Sequence of numbers

- Knowing ordinal and positional language
- Ordering numbers to at least 20
- Counting forward and back within 100
- Counting on from one number to another
- Counting back from one number to another
- Counting on by a stated number
- Counting back by a stated number
- Counting in twos to at least 10
- Counting in tens to 100
- Counting silently in the head
- Counting in fives

Counting items

- Quickly recognizing small quantities without counting (subitizing)
- Counting real objects, in ones and twos
- Counting pictures
- Counting things they cannot touch
- Counting sounds
- Counting physical actions and movements
- Counting imaginary items in their head
- Estimating small quantities

Numerals

- Writing numbers to at least 20
- Recognizing number words
- Matching quantities and numerals
- Knowing structure of 2-digit numbers

Calculations

- Knowing number bonds within 10
- Knowing complements of numbers within 10
- Counting on by small numbers
- Counting back by small numbers
- Knowing doubles to 10
- Knowing 'one more than' and '10 more than' numbers within 100
- Using simple mental strategies for adding and subtracting

Development of activities

The following shows the development of different types of participatory activities within the book. Whenever these activities are used the scope and range can be extended.

Big Circle time

pages: 12, 21, 29, 31, 34
- Counting forward and back to 20
- Number pairs to 10 and doubles
- Counting in twos to 20
- Counting forward and back in tens to 100
- Counting in twos, fives and tens

Show me

pages: 14, 24, 27, 41
- Numeral recognition and order to 20
- Number bonds, language and facts for 0–12
- Teen numbers
- Adding and subtracting to and from teens
- Days of the week

Elastic band strips

pages: 22, 23
- Estimating number position on marked strips within 0–10
- Estimating number position on blank strips within 0–10

Plant pot numbers

pages: 18, 20
- Quick recognition of quantities to 5
- Complements of different numbers to 10

Pendulum count

pages: 13, 29, 30, 34, 37
- Counting within 20
- Counting in twos
- Counting in tens
- Counting in fives and tens
- Counting equal steps

Handfuls

pages: 19, 22, 36
- Quick recognition of quantities to 5
- Number bonds to 5
- Estimation of quantity
- Estimating and sharing
- Putting in twos

0–99 grid

pages: 30, 32, 35, 38
- Tens numbers
- Patterns of tens numbers
- Recognizing 2-digit numbers
- Adding and subtracting 1 and 10
- Patterns of 5 and 10
- Counting on 9 within 0–99

Maths washing lines

pages: 15, 27, 31
- Recognizing and ordering numbers 0–20
- Counting on and back from teens
- Order and recognition of tens numbers

Counting stick

pages: 13, 28, 30, 33, 35
- Counting on and back within 20
- Counting on and back in twos to 20
- Counting on and back in tens to 100
- Counting on and back in fives
- Counting on from 2-digit numbers
- Counting in twos, fives and tens

Flip-flops

pages:19, 20
- Quick recognition of small quantities
- Quick counting within 10
- Complements to 10
- Making totals to 15

Finger flash

pages: 18, 39
- Quick recognition of quantities to 5
- Complements to 5
- Number doubles to 10

Number tracks

pages: 17, 24, 28, 35, 36, 38
- Ordinal numbers to 20
- Counting on and back within 10
- Counting on and back in twos to 20
- Odd and even numbers to 20
- Making equal jumps to 100
- Reaching stated numbers in equal jumps
- Counting on 9 within 0–100

Arrow cards

pages: 26, 32
- Structure of teen numbers
- Adding and subtracting to and from teens
- Adding tens to teens
- Tens and units
- Adding and subtracting 1 and 10 to and from 2-digit numbers

Individual numbers

pages: 15, 21
- Ordering numerals 0–20
- Number pairs to 10 and doubles

Timetable menus

The following pages show a possible activities timetable for the whole year.

The importance of immediate recall of addition and subtraction bonds to 20 cannot be overstated. A short daily dose within the mental maths activities of + and − facts is recommended.

Autumn Term

Week 1
Counting and properties of number 0-20
Big Circle time	*page 12*
Silent counting	*page 12*
Counting stick	*page 13*

Week 2
Counting, language and structure of number
Pendulum count	*page 13*
Human number line	*page 14*
Show me	*page 14*

Week 3
Ordering numbers and simple problem solving
Maths washing line	*page 15*
Individual numbers	*page 15*
Queues	*page 16*
Line up	*page 16*

Week 4
Ordering and quick counting
Number track	*page 17*
Cube towers	*page 17*
Say it quickly	*page 18*
Plant pot numbers	*page 18*

Week 5
Quick counting and number bonds to 5
Finger flash	*page 18*
Flip-flops	*page 19*
Handfuls	*page 19*

Week 6
Number pairs to 10
Flip-flop	*page 20*
Plant pot numbers	*page 20*
Caterpillar	*page 21*
Individual numbers	*page 21*

Week 7
Number pairs to 10
Flip-flop	*page 20*
Plant pot numbers	*page 20*
Caterpillar	*page 21*
Individual numbers	*page 21*

Week 8
Complements to 10 and estimates within 10
Big circle time	*page 21*
Handfuls	*page 22*
Elastic band strip	*page 22*
Elastic band strip	*page 23*

Week 9
Estimates and number facts to 10
Elastic band strip	*page 23*
Rod lengths	*page 23*
Feely box	*page 23*
Show me	*page 24*
Number tracks	*page 24*

Week 10
Complements and number facts to 10
Caterpillar	*page 21*
Individual numbers	*page 21*
Show me	*page 24*
Number tracks	*page 24*

Week 11
Number facts to 10
Show me	*page 24*
Number tracks	*page 24*
Action cards	*page 25*
Tell me about	*page 25*

Week 12
Number facts to 10
Show me	*page 24*
Number tracks	*page 24*
Action cards	*page 25*
Tell me about	*page 25*

Spring Term

Summary Term

Week 1		Week 7	
Counting patterns		**Beginning division**	
Pendulum count	*pages 13, 29, 30*	Handfuls	*page 36*
Counting stick	*pages 13, 28, 30, 33*	Number tracks	*page 36*
Big Circle time	*pages 12, 29, 31*	Stand and sit	*page 36*
Week 2		**Week 8**	
Ordering		**Beginning division**	
Human number line	*page 14*	Pendulum count	*page 37*
Maths washing line	*pages 15, 31*	Number tracks	*page 36*
Number track	*page 17*	Stand and sit	*page 36*
		Circle count	*page 37*
Week 3			
Numbers to 100 and place value		**Week 9**	
Arrow cards	*pages 26, 32*	**Adding 9 and other calculations**	
Counting stick	*page 30*	Pendulum count	*page 30*
0–99 grid	*page 30*	Number tracks	*page 38*
		0–99 grid	*pages 30, 38*
Week 4		Finger flash	*page 39*
Number bonds and calculations		Cube snap	*page 39*
Show me	*page 24*		
Action cards	*page 25*	**Week 10**	
0–99 grid	*page 32*	**Halves, doubles; time**	
In the head	*page 33*	Paper chain	*page 39*
		Cube snap	*page 39*
Week 5		Days of the week	*page 40*
Beginning multiplication		Times	*page 41*
Pendulum count	*page 34*		
Big Circle time	*page 34*	**Week 11**	
Number track	*page 35*	**Time**	
		Days of the week	*page 40*
Week 6		Birthdays	*page 40*
Beginning multiplication		Times	*page 41*
Big Circle time	*page 34*		
Number track	*page 35*	**Week 12**	
0–99 grid	*page 35*	**Time**	
Counting stick	*page 35*	Show me	*page 41*
		Seasons	*page 41*
		Times	*page 41*

As well as trying these suggestions for each term, re-visit other activities for practice, reinforcement and enjoyment.

Resources

To ensure full pupil participation in mental maths activities, a few simple and inexpensive materials are needed. These should be readily available for teacher and pupil use. The materials suggested are used frequently during the activities, and so could form the basis of a mental maths kit.

Counting stick

- A counting stick is a length of wood marked off into ten equal sections either with alternate colours or with coloured tape used to make the divisions. The length is arbitrary, although an unnumbered metre stick marked in decimetres is ideal.

- Another possibility is a length of broom handle with marks made with coloured tape.

Number cards

These are simply numbers copied on to thin card for pupils to hold. Two sizes of number are needed:

- A set of large numbers for class use in *Human number lines* and *Maths washing line* activities.

- Sets of smaller cards for each individual pupil to use in *Show me* tasks.

The number range of a pupil's individual set will begin at 0–5 and extend to 0–20 over a period of time. These number cards can be made using the photocopiable page 42.

Large number cards for human lines

Small number cards for holding up

Flip-flops

Two types of flip-flop are needed: one inexpensive and quickly produced for each pupil and a more substantial one for teacher use.

- The individual pupil flip-flops can be as simple as a photocopy of page 43 on to thin card or paper and folded to show different quantities.

- The teacher flip-flop consists of 16 squares of card sandwiched between two layers of transparent sticky backed film. Leave about 1 cm between the squares to allow for ease of folding. The squares should be about 5 cm.

Some of the squares have pictures stuck on them, typically between seven and ten, although ten is the more usual. Pictures cut from wrapping paper offer an inexpensive source of illustration.

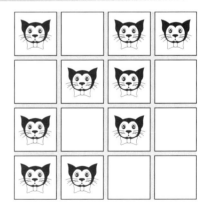

A teacher's flip-flop showing 9

Maths washing lines

Interactive number lines can be made by clipping number cards on to a short length of washing line.

The lines are used in three ways in this book.

- Empty line – pupils clip the numbers on to the line with a clothes peg or bulldog clip. This develops ideas of position.

Empty line – pupils peg numbers on in position

- Pegged line – pegs are already in position on the line for pupils to clip numbers to. This develops counting on and back.

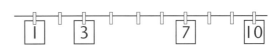

Pegged line – pupils fasten to correct peg

- Numbered lines – with numbers already fastened to the line. Pupils mark the position of numbers with a ring or they turn the number round.

Numbered line – pupils indicate a number by turning it round or placing a ring over the peg

Classroom resources

Commonly available resources are mentioned in the activity notes, with simple alternatives given where appropriate. The following are the main resources required.

- Countable items — Any small objects suitable for rearranging, moving and counting. These can include Linking Elephants, Compare Bears, Playmobile, farm animals or counters.

- Interlocking cubes — These include Multilink cubes or Unifix cubes. The different types of commonly used number tracks can also be utilized during some of the activities.

- Classroom numbers — – Playground painted number tracks and hopscotch markings.
  – Matchbox number lines, school-produced number tracks and grids.
  – Commercial number ladders, tracks, carpet squares, number pockets.

Ready-made resources

Number cards are available from Ginn and Co., Prebendal House, Parson's Fee, Aylesbury, Bucks HP20 2QY.
The following resources are also available from NES Arnold, Ludlow Hill Road, West Bridgeford, Nottingham, NG2 6HD:

- Counting sticks
- Maths washing lines
- Arrow cards
- Elastic band strips
- 'Ele flips' (flip-flops).

Counting forward and back within 20

| Purpose | To check and revise counting words to 20, including number words, counting *forward* and *back* and counting on and back within 0–20. |

Big Circle time *Order of number words forward and back within 20*

Pupils sit in a big circle facing inwards.

◆ Play *Thigh, clap, snap, snap.* Pupils gently slap the top of their thighs with both hands, followed by a clap of both hands. They then snap fingers, first with one hand, then with the other. If they find snapping fingers difficult, this action could be replaced with a brief wave, with alternate hands. Once a rhythm is steady, pupils count from zero to 20 on each 'thigh action', allowing for thinking time during the other actions.

◆ Repeat, except that counting occurs on each action – making it more automatic.

Include several counting cycles of 1–20 with a slight pause between each cycle. Keep the rhythm of the *Thigh, clap, snap, snap* going throughout.

◆ Give a starting number and ask pupils to count on until they reach 20.

◆ Repeat the first three activities for counting back from 20 sequences.

Silent counting *Counting in the head*

Pupils sit at tables, on the mat or in a circle. Ask them to start clapping to a regular, slow rhythm.

◆ They count forward to 20, in time to the clapping but only saying aloud every other number. They 'silent count' alternate numbers.

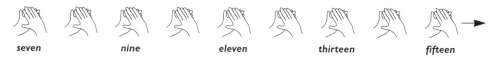

Repeat for counting back from 20, then extend to counting aloud every third number.

Counting stick *Counting on and back within 20*

You will need: a strip of wood, about one metre long, divided into ten sections. An unnumbered decimetre metre stick is ideal.

◆ Choose any number less than 10. Point to one end of the stick and tell pupils that this is the first number on the stick. Then point to each division in turn, asking which number will go there.

Pointing to the divisions

Start from the opposite end of the stick and repeat for counting back within 20.

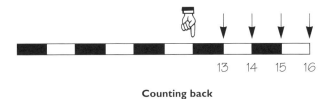

Counting back

Pendulum count *Counting within 20*

You will need: a pendulum, made by fastening a weight to the end of a long piece of string. The pendulum must be fastened so that it swings freely and pupils can count in time with the swings. This sets up a counting rhythm for them to match.

◆ Pupils watch the pendulum swinging and count forward and back within 20.

They should be able to count chunks of number sequences within the 0–20 range.

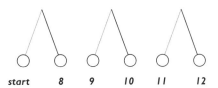
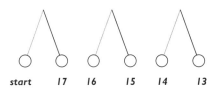

◆ Let the pendulum swing freely. Pupils 'silent count' alternate numbers.

They count forward and back, using different alternate numbers.

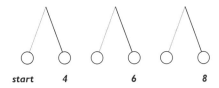
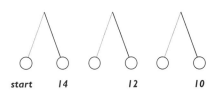

Number language and numerals 0–20

Purpose	To use and correctly order numerals 0–20 and associated number language, including *before, after, next to* and *between*.

Human number line *Positional number language*

You will need: a set of large numeral cards within the range 0–20, ideally with numbers written on the front and back. Whenever pupils are standing and holding these number cards, the order must be correct. They make a number line, either 0–20, or a section of this sequence.

Making a number line

◆ Nominate pupils not holding numbers to go and change places with those holding specified numbers.

Change places with number: 15, 12, 20...
Change places with any number after: 7, 16, 13, 11...
Change places with any number before: 8, 12, 17, 14...
Change places with any number between: 7 and 13, 9 and 16, 14 and 20...
Change places with a number next to: 10, 13, 20, 16...

The pace should be fairly rapid with everyone being called upon, often more than once. Decide whether to use cardinal language. For example:

Change places with a number more than: 5, 13, 19, 11...
Change places with a number less than: 10, 8, 13, 15...
Change places with a number one more than: 9, 13, 16, 19...

Show me *Numeral recognition and order to 20*

You will need: 0–20 number cards (page 42) for each pupil. They should arrange the cards in front of them so that numbers are easily found – either in one line, two lines or in fives.

◆ Pupils hold up number cards to play *Show me*.

Showing numbers in the range 0–20

For example:

Show me number: ten, sixteen, twenty, fourteen....
Show me the number before: nineteen, eleven, six...
Show me the number after: nineteen, nine, fifteen...
Show me any number between: eleven and sixteen, fourteen and twenty...

A quick assessment can be made by glancing round to see the pupils' responses.

Maths washing line *Recognize and order numbers 0–20, including missing numbers*

You will need: a short length of 'washing line' in part of the classroom, consisting of a set of 0–20 numerals and clothes pegs or small bulldog clips for clipping the numbers to the line. Place the numbers in order on the floor or table near to the line.

◆ Pupils choose, or are given, random numbers to clip to the line with a peg. The rule is that all numbers must be in correct sequence when pegged to the line.

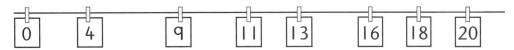

Once all the numbers are in place, ask pupils to remove nominated numbers from the line, then repeat the cycle of adding and removing numbers from the line all over again.

Put on the line: four, sixteen, twenty, eighteen....
Put on the line the number before: fifteen, eleven, three...
Remove from the line the number after: sixteen, eleven, fifteen...
Remove from the line any number between: eleven and sixteen, fourteen and twenty...

Removed numbers should be placed neatly in correct order somewhere near the line.

◆ Clip twenty pegs to the line, ready to accept numbers. Do not use zero in this instance as it can cause confusion. Repeat the first activity but note there is a significant difference this time. Because the pegs are already in position on the line, the pupils have to count on and back to find the correct places for the numbers.

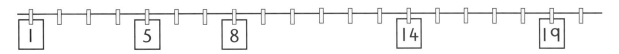

Individual numbers *Ordering numbers 0–20*

You will need: 0–20 number cards (page 42) for each pupil.

◆ Pupils should arrange the cards in front of them in correct order from zero to 20. They should then shuffle or mix up the cards before arranging them in order from 20 to zero. Discuss how numbers can be arranged from smallest to largest and from largest to smallest.

At the end of each lesson, pupils should mix up this set of cards. At the start of subsequent lessons, their first task should be to sort out the cards in order.

Assessment points

✔ count forwards from 0 to 20
✔ count backwards from 20
✔ count on within 20
✔ count back within 20

✔ recognize and order the number symbols 0–20
✔ understand language of position

Ordinal numbers

Purpose   To develop the ordinal language of *first, second, third*, including use of *middle, last, next to last,* and the language of position: *before, after, next to.*

Queues *Ordinal and other positional language*

Pupils sit on the mat or at tables.

◆ Explain that the direction in which things face can change the order of those things. For example, Jo can be first or last depending upon which way the queue is facing.

Jo   Liz   Mark   Jo   Liz   Mark

Ask pupils to make a queue, or queues. Use ordinal and positional language, for example:

Tom, stand first in the queue. Mary, you stand second. Alex, stand in front of Denise. Emma, you go last.
Chris, stand anywhere after Jo. Daniel, stand immediately after Ian.
All turn round to face the opposite direction – who is first now? Who is last? Who is in the middle of the queue?

Line up *Ordinal language with three or four items*

You will need: three or four Linking Elephants, Compare Bears, or similar apparatus. The Elephants or Bears are particularly useful because they clearly face in one direction or another, unlike cubes. Pupils sit at tables.

◆ Tell them to make lines of their Elephants or Bears, using ordinal and positional language to describe what they are doing. Once a line is made, the Elephants or Bears can be turned round to face the opposite direction and the relative positions described.

small Elephant last (or third)   **small Elephant first**

If the Elephants are used and linked, turning them round does not affect their ordinal position.

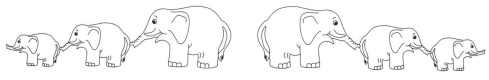

small Elephant first   **small Elephant still first**

Number track *Ordinal numbers to 20*

You will need: Linking Elephants or Compare Bears and a 0–20 number track (page 44). Pupils work in groups or individually. Do not use zero on the track; either colour it in, or place a small straw signpost on it, showing which way to face.

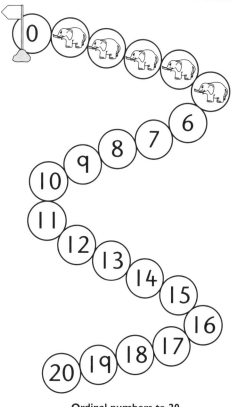

Ordinal numbers to 20

◆ Tell pupils to place a number of Elephants or Bears on the line, all of which face the same way. The first one faces left and the others follow on, like a queue. Discuss which is *first*, *last*, *second*, *third...* Tell them to add more to their line and ask *Which is last now?* Ask about the ordinal positions of different Elephants or Bears: *Put your finger on the: fifth Elephant, eighth Elephant, fifteenth Elephant...*

◆ Tell pupils to place Elephants or Bears in nominated positions: *Put a small green Elephant on the fifth spot. Put a small blue Elephant on the twelfth spot.*

◆ Tell pupils to place Elephants on the first and fifth spots. Ask them to place another Elephant in the *middle*. Talk about the middle position. Repeat the activity to give different middle positions.

Cube towers *Language of position*

You will need: coloured cubes, for example, Multilink or Unifix. Pupils work at tables.

◆ Tell pupils that they are going to be building some towers and that they must follow your instructions. The tower should have red, green, yellow, blue and pink cubes in that order. The red cube should be at the bottom of the tower. Ask which colour is: at the top; at the bottom; in the middle; exactly in the middle. Repeat for different colours and different numbers of cubes.

◆ Talk about the different floors in large shops and high buildings. Tell pupils to make towers and ask them about the first, second, third floors...

Assessment points

✔ know ordinal language to 20
✔ know language of position such as *last* and *middle*

✔ understand positional language such as *between*, *next to* and *after*

Quick counting of small numbers

Purpose	To progress from counting small quantities in ones and to introduce 'subitizing' (recognition of small quantities and number patterns, usually up to 5 or 6).

Say it quickly *Quick recognition of quantities up to 5*

You will need: a set of cards which have spot patterns showing 1–5. Show different patterns for the larger quantities. The spots in each pattern should not be too far apart from each other. A set can be made for use on an overhead transparency.

◆ Show the children the spot patterns in random order. Ask them to say how many spots there are, quite quickly and without apparent counting.

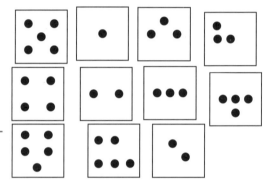

Cards with spot patterns 1–5

Plant pot numbers *Quick recognition of quantities up to 5*

You will need: six counting objects, for example, Linking Elephants or Compare Bears and a small plant pot or similar container.

◆ Cover some of the objects up and ask *Say it quickly, how many can you see?*

Repeat by covering up different numbers of the objects.

As a challenge, ask *How many are hidden?* Pupils can work on this activity in pairs or small co-operating groups, taking turns to cover and count.

How many can you see?

Finger flash *Quick recognition of quantities up to 5 and complements to 5*

Pupils sit at tables, on the mat or in a big circle.

◆ Give them a number. Ask them to quickly flash a number of fingers (using one hand) to match that number. They should not count the fingers in ones.

Quick as a flash, show me: one, two, one, five, three, two, five...

◆ Show pupils a number of fingers up to 5. They then have to show you the correct number of fingers to make 5. In this way, the number pairs which total 5 are being practised.

Flip-flops *Recognizing small quantities and visual counting to 10*

You will need: a demonstration flip-flop, and a flip-flop (page 43) for each pupil.

◆ Fold a flip-flop in different ways to show pupils different quantities between 1 and 10. Ask *How many can you see?* Their responses can be verbal or by holding up a number card.

They should respond more quickly to the small quantities than the larger quantities. Pupils are counting items which they have not touched or moved.

Fold the flip-flop to show different quantities

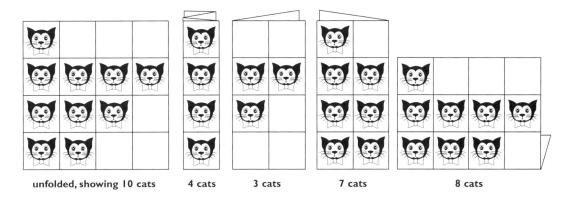

| unfolded, showing 10 cats | 4 cats | 3 cats | 7 cats | 8 cats |

◆ Ask each pupil to fold their own flip-flop to show different quantities.

Show me 5 cats.   Show me 3cats.   Show me 9 cats.

Handfuls *Quick recognition of quantities to 5 and number bonds to 5*

You will need: five small objects for each pupil, for example, counters or pennies. Pupils sit in twos or threes.

◆ They take turns to put some of the five counters in one hand and the rest in the other. Each child then opens one hand to show that quantity, another says how many he can see, without counting in ones, and how many he thinks are in the closed hand.
The first child then opens the closed hand.

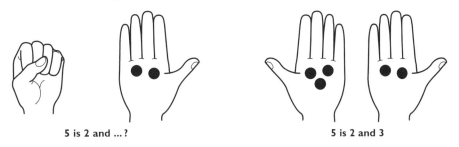

5 is 2 and ... ?   5 is 2 and 3

Assessment points
✔ quickly recognize small quantities without counting in ones   ✔ quick recall of addition facts within 5

Number pairs to 10

> **Purpose** To develop the recall of number pairs and complements of 10, including doubles of numbers to 10 and simple number bond work.

Flip-flops *Complements to 10*

You will need: a demonstration flip-flop, and a flip-flop (page 43) for each pupil.

◆ Fold a flip-flop in different ways to show pupils different quantities between 1 and 10. Ask *How many cats can you see?* followed by *How many cats can I see?* The pupils' responses can be verbal or they can hold up a number card to show how many.

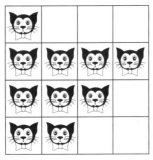

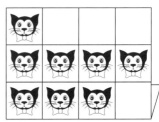

How many cats can I see?

unfolded flip-flop   How many cats can you see?

◆ Pupils work in pairs, each child has a flip-flop. One pupil folds a flip-flop to show a number of cats. The other then has to fold a flip-flop so that the total is 10 cats. The children should take turns in going first. The total number of cats can be changed from 10 to any total between 7 and about 15. Children can also work in threes – making three numbers to create the given totals.

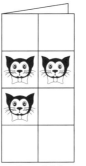 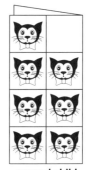

first child   second child
Total of 10 cats

Plant pot numbers *Complements of numbers*

You will need: up to ten counting objects such as Linking Elephants, or Compare Bears and a small plant pot or similar container.

◆ Cover some of them up and ask *How many can you see?* Then ask *How many are hidden?* Change the number of objects being covered up. Pupils can work on this activity in pairs or small co-operating groups, taking turns to cover some of the Elephants.

If there are 10 Elephants, how many are hiding?

Caterpillar *Complements to 10*

You will need: a simple 'caterpillar', or similar, with ten sections, drawn on card; a 'leaf' to cover up a few of the sections.

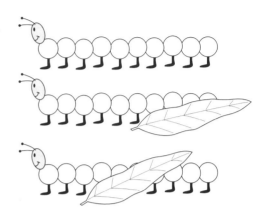

How many feet are hiding?

◆ Children count the feet on the caterpillar and agree that there are ten. Cover some of them up with a paper leaf and ask *How many feet are hiding?* Discuss ways of working this out. If there are several caterpillars, then children can work in small groups with pupils taking turns to cover up some of the feet. Caterpillars can be drawn with different numbers of feet.

This activity acts as a good lead-in to missing number sums such as:
$4 + * = 10$ $* + 2 = 10$ $10 - * = 6$.

Individual numbers *Number pairs to 10 and doubles*

You will need: a set of 0–10 number cards (page 42) for each pupil.

◆ Children place their numbers in order. They find pairs of numbers which have a total of 10. Talk about pairs of numbers which make 10 and how they can be organized.

For example: (10,0) (9,1) (8,2) (7,3) (6,4) (5,5)

If only one set of numbers is used, 5 will not have a partner. Explain how 5 is special and needs a double. Discuss other doubles such as: 2 and 2, 3 and 3... Pairs which make other totals can be found.

◆ Children work in small groups of twos and threes with two sets of numbers 0–10 placed face down in front of them in a random, mixed up order. They take turns to turn over two cards. If the pair totals 10, they keep them, otherwise the cards are replaced and put face down.

Big Circle time *Number pairs to 10 and doubles of numbers to 5*

Pupils sit in a big circle facing inwards. 'Halve' the circle into two teams.

◆ Point to one team member who gives any number in the 0–10 range. Then point to a member in the opposing team who has to give the complement which makes 10. Check that each team has its fair share of going first.

Doubles and other complementary pairs can be done in the same way.

Assessment points

✔ recall of number pairs for 10
✔ know complements for 10
✔ know doubles within 10

✔ quick recall of some complements within 10

Estimating small numbers

Purpose	To estimate quantities and positions of numbers, with emphasis on the latter.
Development	Rounding numbers *to the nearest*.

Handfuls *Estimating a given quantity*

You will need: containers of small objects (for example, counters, beans, centicubes, washers) for each group of pupils.

◆ Tell pupils that this activity is not about 'counting' but about making a 'good guess'. They should each take a handful of items so that they have about six in their hand. They then count to check. If they took five, six or seven, then that was pretty good.

Repeat for different quantities between four and ten.

Handfuls *Estimating how many in a set*

You will need: containers of small objects, as in the previous activity. Pupils sit in twos or threes with a container for each group.

◆ They take turns to place one or two handfuls of objects in front of their partner who has to estimate how many there are. The estimate is checked by counting. For larger quantities, encourage counting in twos. Many children can become anxious over correctness and try to count the set to make sure their 'estimate' is spot on. Reassure them that getting within two or three of the actual total can be a very good estimate indeed.

◆ One pupil takes a quantity of objects out of the container and places them on the table. The other has to put them into two equal piles by estimating rather than by counting. The estimate is then checked and adjusted. Ask *Who is a good sharer?*

Elastic band strip *Estimating position on a marked number strip*

You will need: for each pupil, a strip of card on which is threaded an elastic band that is tight enough not to drop off the strip. The size of each strip is arbitrary but it must be divided into ten sections. Pupils sit at tables or on the mat.

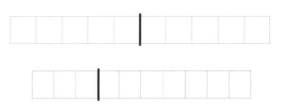

Each card strip has ten divisions and an elastic band

◆ Tell pupils that one end of the strip is zero and the other 10. Their challenge is to move the elastic band quickly along to where they think 5 would be. They then hold up their responses to show you. Discuss the responses and how it can be checked by counting the marks.

Repeat for showing the position of numbers such as: 9, 1, 8, 2...

Elastic band strip *Estimating position on an unmarked number strip*

As for the previous activity. The size of each strip is arbitrary but it must be totally blank.

Each card strip is blank and has an elastic band threaded on it

◆ Tell pupils that one end of the strip is zero and the other 10. Their challenge is to move the elastic band quickly along to where they think 5 would be. Ask them to hold up their responses to show you.

Repeat for showing the position of other numbers, for example: 9, 1, 8, 2...

Rod lengths *Estimating size of numbers by length*

You will need: a collection of number rods such as Multilink Number Rods or Cuisenaire Rods. Home made card strips representing 1 to 10 in length can be used as a substitute. A jumbled collection in a tidy tray is better than using compartmentalized trays. Pupils sit in groups.

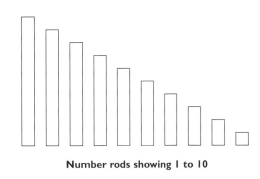

Number rods showing 1 to 10

◆ Explain that the shortest rod is 1. Can they find it and hold it up? The longest rod is a 10. Can they find it and hold it up? By a quick estimate, can they find the rod which they think is a: 9, 5, 2, 7...?

Discuss ways of checking the results.

Feely box *Estimating and approximating lengths*

You will need: a set of number rods and a 'feely bag' or box. Inside the feely bag or box should be ten rods or strips representing 1 to 10 in length. Pupils sit in groups.

◆ Hold up one of the number rods. Ask pupils to take turns to feel inside their box and to find a rod which is the same. This they take out to check. Repeat for different lengths of rods.

◆ Hold up a number rod. Ask pupils to find and take out of the feely box a rod which is longer. In their descriptions, they should use the language of approximation and estimation for example, *shorter, a little bit longer, a lot shorter, very nearly the same but not quite.*

Number facts to 10

Purpose	To practise the number bonds within 10, use number facts (for example, odd and even) and the language of number.
Development	Using number facts beyond 10.

Show me *Number bonds, language and facts within 0–12*

You will need: a set of 0–12 number cards (page 42) for each pupil. They should arrange the cards in front of them so that numbers are easily found.

◆ Play *Show me* with addition facts.

Showing two numbers which total 10

Show me two numbers which total: 10, 9, 6...
What is 2 more than: 4, 6, 7, 8...?
What is the total of: 3 and 4, 5 and 5, 0 and 4...?
What is double: 5, 3, 6...?

◆ Play *Show me* with subtraction facts.

What is 2 less than: 10, 3, 2, 5...?
What is 6 take away 3?
Show me which number will make this number total ten: 3, 6, 4...
What is 3 less than: 4, 10, 5, 7...

◆ Play *Show me* with number facts.

Show me an odd number.
Show me an even number which is more than 5.
Show me a number which is between 3 and 9.

For a quick assessment, glance round at the pupils' responses.

Number tracks *Counting on and back from various numbers*

You will need: a 0–20 number track (page 44) and a marker for moving along the track for each pupil.

◆ Pupils place their marker on a nominated number and move it forwards a given number of hops.

Put your marker on 3. Make 5 hops forward. Where will it land?
What is 5 more than 3?
Put your marker on 5. Make 2 hops forward. Where will it land?
What is 2 more than 5?

Repeat for different hops forward from various numbers.

◆ Pupils place their marker on a nominated number and move it back a given number of hops.

Put your marker on 7. Make 5 hops back. Where will it land? What is 5 less than 7?
Put your marker on 8. Make 2 hops back. Where will it land? What is 2 less than 8?

Repeat for different hops back from various numbers.

Action cards *Number bonds, language and facts within 0–10*

You will need: a line of numbers 0–10 on the floor and a set of 'action cards'. Action cards have sums, number language and number facts written on them. The choice of card should be appropriate for the level of specific pupils.

◆ Choose an action card and read it with the children. Discuss which number, or numbers, that action card could go on. Sometimes only one number is possible, as with '2 more than 5'. On other occasions, there are several possibilities, as with 'an even number'. The action card is placed on an appropriate number and the next one discussed.

addition and subtraction facts	language of position	number facts
2 more than 5	the number after 7	an even number
4 add 5	any number after 6	an odd number
double 3	a number next to 8	
2 + 7	a number between 5 and 9	
1 less than 6	a number before 4	

Examples of action cards

◆ When all the action cards have been placed, each number will most likely have several on it. Choose one of these numbers and its action cards. Ask pupils to give number sentences about that number. For instance:

Six is double 3. Six is an even number. Six is a number between 5 and 9. Six is five add one. Six is 2 more than 4.

◆ Groups of pupils could take a number and its action cards and write number sentences in their books.

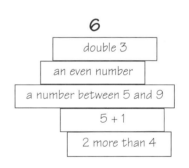

Number 6 with a range of action cards

Tell me about *Number language*

Pupils sit in a large circle, at tables or on the mat.

◆ Choose any starting number between 0 and 10. Pupil take turns to give a fact about that number. They should not repeat what anyone else has said although variations are allowed if different number language is used.

What can you tell me about 6? It is double 3. It is 1 less than 7. It is 6 add zero. It is 2 more than 4.

Allow more general number language to be used as well.

It comes between 5 and 7. It is a number before ten. It is the tens number in sixty.

Teen numbers

Purpose To develop understanding of the structure of numbers between 10 and 20, and to make simple calculations with teens (including 11 and 12).

Arrow cards *Learning the structure of the teen numbers*

You will need: (ideally) a demonstration set of tens and units arrow cards (page 46), and a set for each pupil.

◆ Show pupils how to make 16 with arrow cards and that it is a 10 and a 6. Now ask them to make a range of teen numbers with their arrow cards. This will help them to see how different teen numbers are constructed.

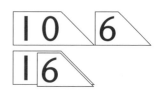

Arrow cards making 16

◆ Tell pupils to make a teen number such as 17. Ask what are you left with if you take away 10 from this number. Repeat for taking away 10 from other teen numbers. Now do the activity but take away the unit figure.
Make 14. Take away 4. What are you left with?

Arrow cards *Adding and subtracting small numbers to and from teen numbers*

You will need: a set of tens and units arrow cards (page 46) for each pupil.

◆ Tell each pupil to make a teen number such as 13. Ask them to add 4 to this number and to show you the answer. Point out that they are only changing the units (or ones) number. In the same way, tell them to add and subtract small numbers to and from a range of teen numbers. As a challenge, see if pupils can quickly add and subtract small numbers from teens without using the arrow cards.

13 add on 4

Arrow cards *Adding tens to teen numbers*

You will need: a set of tens and units arrow cards (page 46) for each pupil.

◆ Tell each pupil to make a teen number such as 13. Ask them to add 10 to this number and to show you the answer. Note that they are only changing the tens number. In the same way, tell pupils to add other tens to a range of teen numbers. As a challenge, see if pupils can quickly add tens to teens without using the arrow cards. They can use their fingers to check the tens being counted.

Adding 10 to a teen number

Show me *Recording teen numbers*

You will need: (ideally) a set of demonstration digit cards and a set of digit cards for each pupil (use part of set on page 42).

◆ Explain how to make a teen number from two cards. Show how to hold them as a fan in one hand. Play *Show me* activities where the pupils make nominated teen numbers and hold them up. Some pupils will reverse the digits, such as showing 51 rather than 15. *Show me: fifteen, eleven, nineteen, twelve...*

Two digit cards making 15

Show me *Adding and subtracting small numbers to and from teen numbers*

You will need: (ideally) a demonstration set of 0–20 number cards and a set (see page 42) for each pupil.

◆ Give pupils a range of problems which involve adding and subtracting small numbers to and from teen numbers. They hold up number cards to show their answers. The success rate can be gauged by a glance round.

Show me 2 more than 15. Show me 16 add on 3.
Show me 3 less than 16. Show me 19 take away 2.

Maths washing line *Counting on and back from teen numbers*

You will need: a short length of 'washing line'; a set of 0–20 number cards (page 42), pegged to the line; a plastic ring, or other suitable marker.

◆ Hang the ring on a teen number. Ask nominated pupils to come and move the ring forwards or backwards as appropriate.

Part of a maths washing line with 14 marked

Add on 2. Which number will be ringed?
Take away 4. Which number will be ringed?
Ring the number which is one more than 15.
Ring the number which is two less than 16.

Assessment points

✔ know the structure of teen numbers   ✔ subtract small numbers from teens
✔ add small number to teens   ✔ add and subtract 10 to and from teens

---

Counting in twos

Purpose	To count on and back in twos, to at least 20, including odd and even numbers.
Development	Counting beyond 20.

Counting stick *Counting on and back to 20 in twos*

You will need: a counting stick – a strip, about one metre long, divided into ten sections. An unnumbered decimetre metre stick is ideal.

◆ Point to one end of the stick and say that zero goes there. Point to the other end and say that 20 goes there. Tell pupils that they are going to count in twos.
Point to each division from zero to 20 in turn, asking which number will go there. Point to each division from 20 to zero in turn, asking which number will go there.
It is important for pupils to know that zero does not have the property of a number, so it is not an even, or odd number.

Name the ends of the stick.

0   20

Point to each division in turn, forward and back.

0 2 4 6 8 10 12
count forward ⟶

8 10 12 14 16 18 20
⟵ count back

Number track *Counting on and back in twos/Odd and even numbers*

You will need: for each pupil, a 0–20 number track (page 44) and a small object, such as a Linking Elephant or Compare Bear, to move along the track.

◆ Tell each pupil to place their Elephant on zero and to imagine that it jumps along in twos. Ask where it would land in: three jumps, five jumps, two jumps…

Next, ask them to place the Elephant on 1. Ask where it will land now in: three jumps, five jumps, two jumps…

◆ As for the first activity, ask where the Elephant would land if it started on higher numbers and jumped back in twos.

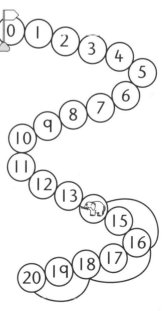

Counting back in twos

Big Circle time *Counting in twos forward to 20*

Pupils sit in a big circle facing inwards.

◆ Play *Thigh, clap, snap, snap*. Pupils gently slap the top of their thighs with both hands, followed by a clap of both hands. They then snap their fingers, first with one hand, then with the other. If they find snapping difficult, then they can wave instead, using alternate hands. Once a rhythm is steady, they count up to 20 in twos on the 'thigh action', allowing for thinking time during the other actions.

◆ Extend the first activity by counting in twos on each action.

Discuss even numbers between zero and 20 and how they always end in 0, 2, 4, 6 or 8.

◆ Repeat the previous two activities by counting on in twos from 1 to generate the odd numbers. Discuss odd numbers between zero and 20 and how they always end in 1, 3, 5, 7 or 9.

If appropriate, extend counting in twos beyond 20.

Pendulum count *Counting in twos*

You will need: a pendulum, made from a weight and string. The pendulum must be fastened so that it swings freely and pupils can count in time with the swings. This sets up a counting rhythm for them to match.

◆ Pupils watch the pendulum swinging and count forward and back in twos. Start the count with 2 and go beyond 20 if it seems appropriate. Then start the count at 1 and count in twos.

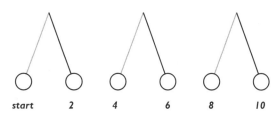

Assessment points

✔ count forwards in twos   ✔ know odd numbers to 20
✔ count backwards in twos   ✔ know even numbers to 20

Counting in tens

Purpose	To count forward and back in tens and to learn the decade numbers: 10, 20, 30... 100.

Counting stick *Counting on and back to 100 in tens*

You will need: a counting stick – a strip, about one metre long, divided into ten sections. An unnumbered decimetre metre stick is ideal.

◆ Point to one end of the stick and say that zero goes there. Point to the other end and say that 100 goes there. Tell pupils that they are going to count in tens. Point to each division from zero to 100 in turn, asking which number will go there. Pupils count 10, 20, 30... Point to each division from 100 to zero in turn, asking which number will go there. Pupils count 90, 80, 70...

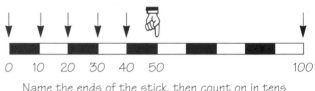

Name the ends of the stick, then count on in tens

Name the ends of the stick, then count back in tens

Pendulum count *Counting in tens*

You will need: a pendulum, made from a weight and swing. The pendulum must be fastened so that it swings freely and pupils can count in time with the swings. This sets up a rhythm against which pupils can match their counting.

◆ Pupils watch the pendulum swinging and count forward and back in tens. Start the count with zero and go beyond 100 if it seems appropriate. Then start the count at 100 and count back in tens. If, initially, the swing is too quick, lengthen the pendulum to slow it down.

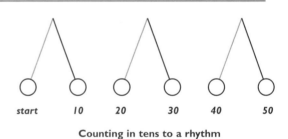

Counting in tens to a rhythm

0–99 grid *Recognizing tens numbers and looking for patterns*

You will need: a 0–99 grid (page 47) and a marker for each pupil.

◆ Tell pupils to place their marker on each of the tens numbers in turn. What do they notice? Choose random tens numbers and tell them to place a marker on them to check whether they recognize the numeral. Ask what tens numbers always end in. Decide whether to use the word 'digit'.

0	1	2	3	4	5	6	7	8	9
10	11	12	13	14	15	16	17	18	19
20	21	22	23	24	25	26	27	28	29
30	31	32	33	34	35	36	37	38	39
40	41	42	43	44	45	46	47	48	49
50	51	52	53	54	55	56	57	58	59
60	61	62	63	64	65	66	67	68	69
70	71	72	73	74	75	76	77	78	79
80	81	82	83	84	85	86	87	88	89
90	91	92	93	94	95	96	97	98	99

Big Circle time *Counting in tens forward and back within 100*

Pupils sit in a big circle facing inwards.

◆ Play *Thigh, clap, snap, snap.* Pupils gently slap the top of their thighs with both hands, followed by a clap of both hands. They then snap fingers, first with one hand, then with the other. If they find snapping fingers difficult, they could wave with alternate hands. Once a rhythm is steady, pupils count up to 100 in tens on each 'thigh action', the other actions allowing for thinking time.

Extend this to counting on each of the actions not just on the 'thigh action'. When pupils are confident, include counting back in tens.

◆ Include counting on and back by a given number of tens. For example:

Count on three tens from 40. Count back two tens from 80.

Maths washing lines *Order and recognition of the tens numbers to 100*

You will need: a short length of 'washing line' fastened up in part of the classroom; clothes pegs or small bulldog clips for clipping the numbers to the line; a set of tens numbers 0, 10, 20... 100. Place the numbers in order on the floor or table near to the line.

◆ Pupils choose, or are given, random tens numbers to clip to the line with a peg. The rule is that all numbers must be in correct sequence when pegged to the line. This activity uses ideas of position and estimating where the numbers go.

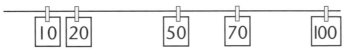

◆ Fasten ten pegs to the line. Pupils clip tens numbers on to appropriate pegs. This activity will involve pupils in counting on and back in tens to find the correct peg for each number.

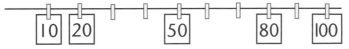

As an extension, include discussion as to where numbers in between the tens numbers would go. For example:

Where would 45 go? What is the position of 99?

Assessment points
✔ count forwards in tens
✔ count backwards in tens
✔ recognize tens numbers when written
✔ order tens numbers

Numbers to 100

Purpose	To count on and back by 1 and 10 and in steps of 5; to add and subtract small numbers to and from 2-digit numbers.

Arrow cards *Adding and subtracting 1 and 10 to and from 2-digit numbers*

You will need: a set of tens and units arrow cards (page 46) and (ideally) a demonstration set of these.

◆ Show how a number such as 36 is made up of 30 and 6. Refer to the digit 3 as being 30 rather than three tens.

Give pupils a range of 2-digit numbers to make using their arrow cards.

Show me: 38, 75, 81, 57...

Through making different numbers with the arrow cards, pupils will see how 2-digit numbers are constructed.

30 6

36

Arrow cards making 36

◆ Explain how to find numbers which are 1 more and 1 less by counting on or back.

Show me 46. Make it 1 more and show me the answer.
Show me 59. Make it 1 more and show me the answer.
Show me 84. Make it 1 less and show me the answer.
Show me 70. Make it 1 less and show me the answer.

◆ Explain how to find numbers which are 10 more and 10 less by counting on or back.

Show me 25. Make it 10 more and show me the answer.
Show me 34. Make it 10 less and show me the answer.

0–99 grid *Recognizing 2-digit numbers/Adding and subtracting ones and tens*

You will need: a 0–99 grid (page 47) and a marker for each pupil.

◆ Tell pupils to place their marker on some tens numbers. Choose random numbers and tell them to place a marker on them to check whether they recognize the number.

0	1	2	3	4	5	6	7	8	9
10	11	12	13	14	15	16	17	18	19
20	21	22	23	24	25	26	27	28	29
30	31	32	33	34	35	36	37	38	39
40	41	42	43	44	45	46	47	48	49
50	51	52	53	54	55	56	57	58	59
60	61	62	63	64	65	66	67	68	69
70	71	72	73	74	75	76	77	78	79
80	81	82	83	84	85	86	87	88	89
90	91	92	93	94	95	96	97	98	99

◆ Pupils place their marker on a number such as 48. Tell them to add on 1 and move the marker to the new number. Repeat for taking away 1. Tell them to pay particular attention to adding 1 to numbers ending in 9 and subtracting 1 from tens numbers.

Similarly, get pupils to add and subtract 10 to and from a range of numbers. Discuss what they notice about any patterns, such as moving vertically down when adding and vertically up when subtracting.

◆ Tell pupils to use the grid to help them add and subtract small numbers such as 2 and 3 from 2-digit numbers. *What is 2 more than 53? What is 3 less than 70?*

Counting stick *Counting on and back in fives/Counting on from 2-digit numbers*

You will need: a counting stick – a strip, about one metre long, divided into ten sections.

◆ Point to one end of the stick and say that zero goes there. Point to the other end and say that 50 goes there. Tell pupils that they are going to count in fives.

Name the ends of the stick, then count on in fives

Point to each division from zero to 50 in turn, asking which number will go there. Pupils count 5, 10, 15, 20...

If appropriate, point to each division from 50 to zero in turn asking which number will go there. Pupils count 50, 45, 40...

Name the ends of the stick, then count back in fives

◆ Choose a random 2-digit starting number such as 32. Point to one end of the stick and say that is 32. Pupils then count on in ones from that number. Similarly, name the other end of the stick with a number such as 87 and ask pupils to count back in ones from that number.

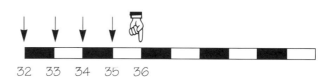

Count on from 2-digit numbers

In the head *Counting on and back from 2-digit numbers*

Pupils sit at tables, on the mat or in a big circle.

◆ Tell pupils that they are going to count on 2 from some numbers. Give a starting number such as 27. Ask them to tap their head when they put in the starting number, then they count on 2 from the number.

27 (tap head) 28 29
65 (tap head) 66 67

Ask pupils to count on small numbers to other 2-digit numbers.

◆ Give a starting number such as 64. Pupils tap their head when they put in the starting number, then they count back 2 from the number.

64 (tap head) 63 62
41 (tap head) 40 39

Beginning multiplication

Purpose	To count on in steps of two, five and ten; to develop ideas of adding 'lots of'.

Pendulum count *Counting in fives and tens*

You will need: a pendulum, made from a weight and string. The pendulum must be fastened so that it swings freely and pupils can count in time with the swings. This sets up a counting rhythm for them to match.

◆ Pupils watch the pendulum swinging and count forwards in twos, fives and tens. Decide whether to include threes. Start the count with zero and go as far as seems appropriate.
If, initially, the swing is too quick, lengthen the pendulum to slow it down. If pupils count on one of the swings rather than on both of them this will increase the amount of thinking time available to them.

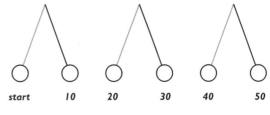

Counting in tens to a rhythm

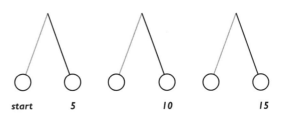

Counting in fives on alternate swings allowing more thinking time

◆ As a challenge, ask children to count forward, for example, for six tens, and then to stop counting. They can use their fingers to check off how many tens have been counted. Change the number of tens which are being counted. Include counting on by a different numbers of fives if it seems appropriate.

Big Circle time *Counting in twos, fives and tens*

Pupils sit in a big circle facing inwards.

◆ Play *Thigh, clap, snap, snap.* Pupils gently slap the top of their thighs with both hands, followed by a clap of both hands. They then snap fingers, first with one hand, then with the other. If they find snapping difficult, this action could be replaced by a brief wave of alternate hands. Once a rhythm is steady, pupils 'silent count' for numbers one through four, saying *five* aloud. They continue, saying aloud all the multiples of five.

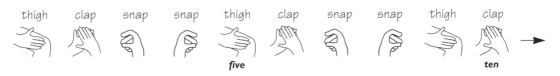

◆ Repeat for counting in tens, twos and, if appropriate, threes.

Number track *Making equal jumps along a number track*

You will need: for each pupil, the 0–100 number track (page 45) and a marker, such as a Linking Elephant or Compare Bear.

◆ Pupils place their marker on zero. Tell them that they are going to make jumps of two. After the first jump, they will be on 2, then 4, then 6, and so on. They should make the jumps along the line with their marker and say aloud which numbers they are landing on. You could clap your hands to show that a jump has to be made. This will help to keep the class together. Decide how far along the line to count in twos.

◆ Repeat the 'jumping along' activity for jumps of ten and five. Use jumps of three if it seems appropriate.

0–99 grid *Looking for patterns of 5 and 10 on a 0–99 grid*

You will need: for each pupil, a 0–99 grid (page 47) and a marker.

◆ Pupils place their marker on zero. Tell them that they are going to make jumps of ten. Ask where the first jump will take them. They should make the jump with their marker. They should not be counting on in ones at this point. Similar jumps of ten down the number grid can be made landing on 20, 30, 40...

Now ask them where they would land if they made four jumps of ten from zero. Similarly, tell them to make different jumps of ten from zero.

◆ Repeat the jumping activity for jumps of five.

Counting stick *Counting on in twos, fives and tens*

You will need: a strip of wood, about one metre long, divided into ten sections. An unnumbered decimetre metre stick is ideal.

◆ Tell pupils which end of the stick is zero and that each jump of your finger is two. Move your finger along the stick and ask them to say the number at which it stops. At first, let them say each number aloud. Then ask them to count silently and only say the number on which your finger finally rests. Finally, as a challenge, ask them to say how many jumps of two you made.

Counting in jumps of two

◆ Repeat for jumps of five and ten along the stick. Ask on which number your finger finally rests.
As in the previous activity, the children can be challenged by being asked to say how many jumps of five or ten you made.

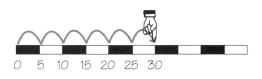

Making six jumps of five

Beginning division

<table>
<tr><td>Purpose</td><td>To repeat 'subtraction' of 2, 5 and 10; to develop ideas about equal groups or 'lots of'.</td></tr>
</table>

Handfuls *Putting into twos*

You will need: cubes or other small objects.

◆ Tell pupils to make a line of eight cubes. Them ask them to take a cube from each end, at the same time, using both hands. The two cubes should then be put neatly together at one side. This is repeated until the complete line has been put into twos. Ask how many twos are in 8.
In the same way, they can put other even numbers into twos, after the important first step of taking two cubes at the same time from the line.

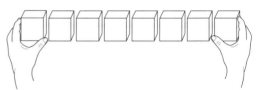

Taking cubes, two at a time, from a line

◆ Similar to the previous activity, except that an odd number of cubes are used. There should always be one cube left over after the pairing activity. Discuss odd and even numbers and remainders.

Number tracks *Counting on in equal jumps to stated numbers*

You will need: a 0–20 number track (page 44) and a marker for moving along the track.

◆ Tell pupils that the marker is going to jump along the track in twos. Ask how many jumps to reach 8. Repeat for other even numbers within the 0–20 range. Tell pupils to place their marker on 12. Ask how many jumps of two it takes to land on zero. Start the marker on other even numbers and tell pupils to make jumps of two to land on zero.

◆ Decide whether to include making equal jumps of three or four.

Stand and sit *Counting in equal steps to reach stated numbers*

Pupils sit on chairs, either at tables, in a big circle or in lines.

◆ Pupils count in unison, alternately standing and sitting for each number in the count. This helps keep a rhythm for the count and allows for a little thinking time. Tell them to count in twos, until they reach 10, and to keep count of how many twos on their fingers.

stand	sit	stand	sit	stand
two	**four**	**six**	**eight**	**ten**

Change the number which has to be reached in twos.
Decide whether to use fives, tens or other size of counting step.

Pendulum count *Counting the number of equal steps*

You will need: a pendulum, made from a weight and string. The pendulum must be fastened so that it swings freely and pupils can count in time with the swings. This sets up a counting rhythm for them to match.

◆ Tell pupils to count forwards in twos in time to the swing. When pupils are confident in counting in twos, tell them to count to 8 in twos. They must also keep a check on how many twos they counted. They can use fingers to keep a tally of the count.

Counting in twos to reach 8

start   2   4   6   8

4 twos reach 8

◆ Tell pupils that they are going to count on for five twos and that they must stop when they have reached the correct number. If they use their fingers as a tally, it will help them keep a check of how many twos have been used. This must be done to the swing of the pendulum.

Counting on for 5 twos

| 1 two | 2 twos | 3 twos | 4 twos | 5 twos |
| two | four | six | eight | ten |

Circle count *Counting forward and back in equal steps*

Pupils stand in two concentric circles of about the same number. If the class is large, they can stand in two or more sets of concentric circles. The inner circle face clockwise and the outer circle face anti-clockwise. Each pupil raises his left hand and walks slowly round gently slapping (or shaking) with the passing person in the other circle. Practise this.

◆ Pupils walk round slapping hands in time to counting forward in twos. When a stated number is reached, each circle reverses direction and pupils raise their right hands to slap and count back in twos to zero. This should be done to a regular rhythm and the change of direction carried out smoothly. A chime bar or tambour can be used to maintain the pace.

Clap round in twos until you reach 16. Then clap back in twos to zero.

◆ Repeat the previous activity but counting forward and back in fives and tens.

Clap round in fives until you reach 35. Then clap back in fives to zero.
Clap round in tens until you reach 70. Then clap back in tens to zero.

◆ This is a little more challenging. As the children pass by, slapping hands, the outer circle counts in twos and the inner circle counts how many twos there are.

Outer circle   *two   four   six   eight   ten   twelve   fourteen*
Inner circle   *one   two three four   five   six   seven*

In the same way, count round in fives and tens.

Adding on 9

Purpose	To teach the strategy of adding on 9 by adding 10, then taking away 1.

Number tracks *Counting on by nines*

You will need: for each pupil, a 0–100 track (page 45) and a marker for jumping along the track.

◆ Begin by checking that the pupils can make jumps of ten along the track starting from any number. They should not count in ones but should know and be able to use the pattern of counting in tens such as 26, 36, 46, 56...

◆ Explain how to count on in nines by making a jump of 10 forward and a hop of 1 back. Give starting numbers from which they can count on by 9. Check that they are not counting in ones.

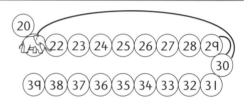

Jump 10 forward and 1 back to count in nines

◆ Ask pupils to make consecutive jumps of 9 from different starting numbers. They can record the sequence of numbers in their books.

0–99 grid *Counting on by nines*

You will need: for each pupil, a 0–99 grid (page 47) and a marker for moving about the grid.

◆ Begin by checking that they can make moves of 10 on the grid starting from any number. They should not count in ones but should know and be able to use the pattern of counting in tens such as 41, 51, 61, 71... Discuss how tens numbers are underneath each other on the grid.

0	1	2	3	4	5	6	7	8	9
10	11	12	13	14	15	16	17	18	19
20	21	22	23	24	25	26	27	28	29
30	31	32	33	34	35	36	37	38	39
40	41	42	43	44	45	46	47	48	49
50	51	52	53	54	55	56	57	58	59
60	61	62	63	64	65	66	67	68	69
70	71	72	73	74	75	76	77	78	79
80	81	82	83	84	85	86	87	88	89
90	91	92	93	94	95	96	97	98	99

Moves of adding on 9 on a 0–99 grid

◆ Explain how to count on in nines by making a move of 10 forward, followed by a move of 1 back. Give starting numbers from which pupils count on by 9. Check that they are not counting in ones.

◆ Ask pupils to make consecutive jumps of 9 from different starting numbers. They can record the sequence of numbers.

Doubles and halves

Purpose	To develop work on doubling and halving, including near doubles.

Finger flash *Learning doubles to 10*

Pupils sit at tables, on the mat or in a big circle, with both hands up looking at their palms.

◆ Choose a number from 1 to 5. Ask them to fold down that number of fingers on each hand.

| 1 and 1 | 2 and 2 | 3 and 3 | 4 and 4 | 5 and 5 |

Ask how many fingers are folded. If the children find this difficult, tell them to look at their unfolded fingers, which may help.

◆ Check whether pupils can recall all doubles to at least 10, without using their fingers.

◆ Tell pupils to show a double such as 2 and 2, then to fold down one more finger to make a near double. What is the new total? Repeat for other near doubles.

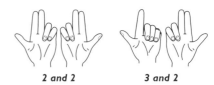

2 and 2   **3 and 2**

Near doubles

Paper chain *Halving and doubling*

You will need: several scissors and one sheet of paper. Pupils sit in a large circle or as a large informal group.

◆ Explain how to fold and cut in half. Tell one pupil to fold and cut the paper in half. He should then give away these two pieces to any two children. They then fold the paper and cut in half and give away the two pieces. This continues until everyone has a piece of paper; discard any left-over pieces.

At the simplest level, this activity develops skills of folding and halving. It could also lead to discussion about doubling and redoubling.

Cube snap *Halving numbers to at least 10*

You will need: interlocking cubes such as Multilink or Unifix for each pupil.

◆ Tell pupils to make a stick from eight cubes. They snap the stick in half and compare the halves to find half of 8. This is repeated for other lengths. Ask which sticks can be halved.

◆ Tell pupils to make a stick from an odd number of cubes. They then snap the sticks into near halves.

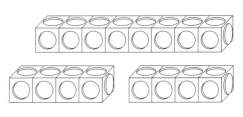

Halving 8

Talking about time

Purpose	To revise the days of the week and months, and telling the time using 'o'clock'.

Birthdays *Learning birthday months*

Pupils sit at tables, on the mat or in a big circle.

◆ They sing a birthday song to the child celebrating and they clap to match the age. Discuss the passing of time and years. Pictures and names of birthday pupils can be stuck to a monthly chart.

◆ Use a birthday chart to show all the months and who has a birthday within each month. Explain how birthdays have a month and day of that month. Children should learn their own birthday month and ideally the day upon which it falls.

'Birthday Song'
(tune of Frère Jacques)
One year older
One year older
5 today
5 today
Have a happy birthday
Have a happy birthday
Celebrate
Celebrate

Days of the week *Learning the names of the days of the week/Morning and afternoon*

You will need: labels showing the days of the week, placed in order. They can be in a line or in a circle showing the cyclical nature of the days of the week.

◆ Remind pupils about the order of the days and how they go round and round. Ask which day it is **today** and show the label. Ask which day it will be **tomorrow** and what it was **yesterday**. Show the labels. Talk about weekends and which days these are. Explain that there seven days in a week. Ask which days are at the start of week and which at the end. Also talk about midweek and school days.

◆ Explain about morning and afternoon and the events which occur in each part of the day. Talk about there being 24 hours in each day.

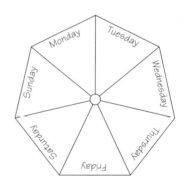

Rotating disc showing days of the week

Show me *Learning about days of the week*

You will need: a set of labels showing the names of the days of the week for each pupil. They could make their own, copying from a wall chart.

◆ Pupils hold up one or more labels in response to your questions. Ask a range of questions such as:

Show me: Monday, Wednesday, Sunday...
Show me the day after: Thursday, Saturday, Tuesday...
Show me the day before: Friday, Sunday, Wednesday...

Seasons *Learning the order and names of the seasons*

You will need: a chart showing the seasons in quadrants to highlight the cyclical nature of seasons.

◆ Ask the children to say the names of the seasons. Talk about what happens in each season. Explain the order of the seasons within each year. See who has a birthday in the summer, autumn, winter or spring.

Times *Recognizing the 'o'clock' times*

You will need: a teaching clock

◆ Talk about the hour hand and the minute hand of a clock. Discuss other clock and watch attributes which the children may have or know about, for example second-hand, winders, date window. Explain how some clocks and watches have digital numbers and others have hands.

With the teaching clock show how 'o'clock' times always have the minute hand on the 12. Show some 'o'clock' times and see if the children can say the time.

◆ Explain that when the minute hand has gone half-way round the clock, it shows half-past. With the teaching clock, show how 'half-past' times always have the minute hand on the 6. Show some 'half-past' times and see if the children can say the time.

◆ If appropriate, talk about one hour *later* and those o'clock times which are one hour later than others. Similarly, talk about there being 60 minutes in one hour and 60 seconds in one minute.

Assessment points

✔ know the names and order of days of the week
✔ know birthday months

✔ know the order of the seasons
✔ recognize some 'o'clock' and 'half-past' times

0–20 Number Cards

0	1	2	3
4	5	6	7
8	9	10	11
12	13	14	15
16	17	18	19
20			

Cut out these number cards.

INTERACTIVE MENTAL MATHS |

Flip-flop

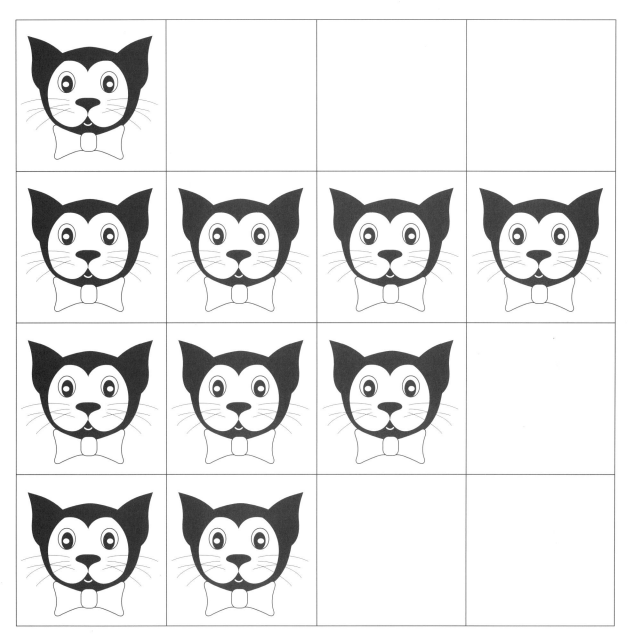

 Cut out the large square and fold along the lines.
Make the creases fold both ways.

INTERACTIVE MENTAL MATHS 1

0-20 Number Track

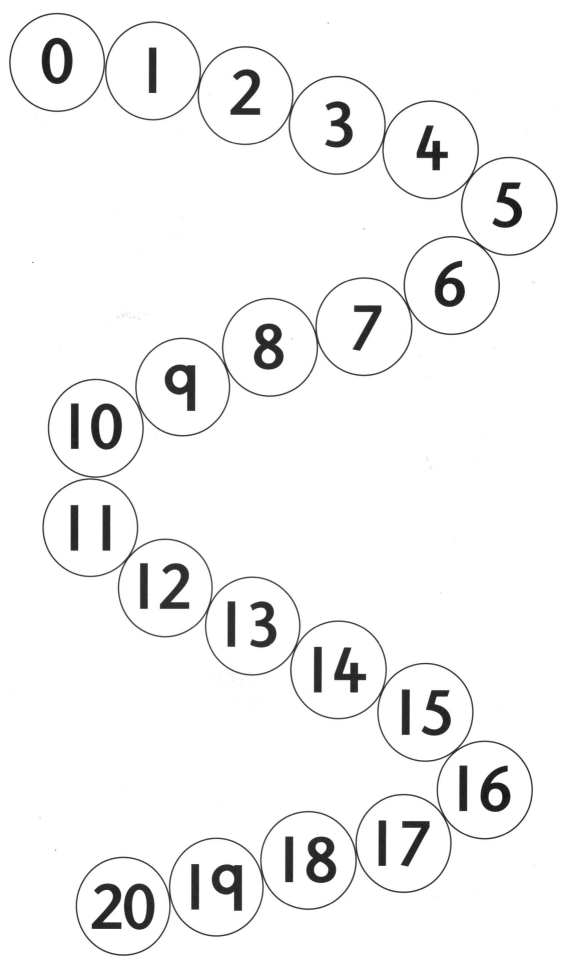

INTERACTIVE MENTAL MATHS | © Peter Patilla 1999. Heinemann Educational Ltd. For copyright restrictions see reverse of title page.

0–100 Number Track

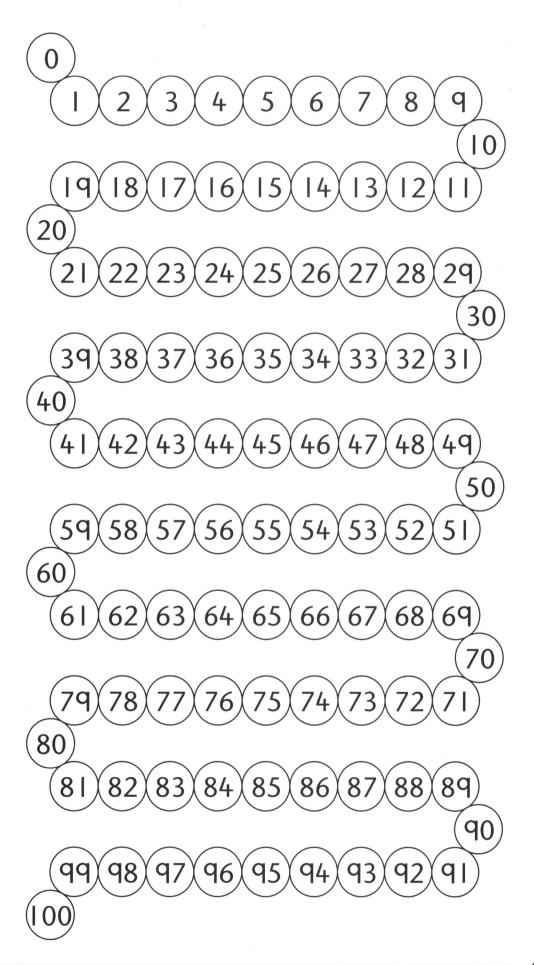

INTERACTIVE MENTAL MATHS I

Tens and Units Arrow Cards

0   1   10

2   3   20

4   5   30

6   7   40

8   9   50

60   70

80   90

100

 INTERACTIVE MENTAL MATHS | © Peter Patilla 1999. Heinemann Educational Ltd. For copyright restrictions see reverse of title page.

0-99 Grid

0	1	2	3	4	5	6	7	8	9
10	11	12	13	14	15	16	17	18	19
20	21	22	23	24	25	26	27	28	29
30	31	32	33	34	35	36	37	38	39
40	41	42	43	44	45	46	47	48	49
50	51	52	53	54	55	56	57	58	59
60	61	62	63	64	65	66	67	68	69
70	71	72	73	74	75	76	77	78	79
80	81	82	83	84	85	86	87	88	89
90	91	92	93	94	95	96	97	98	99